**Hinman, Bonnie
Mississippi**

CORE LIBRARY OF US STATES

MISSISSIPPI

BY BONNIE HINMAN

CONTENT CONSULTANT
Deanne Stephens, PhD
Professor of History
University of Southern Mississippi

Core Library

An Imprint of Abdo Publishing
abdobooks.com

abdobooks.com

Published by Abdo Publishing, a division of ABDO, PO Box 398166, Minneapolis, Minnesota 55439. Copyright © 2023 by Abdo Consulting Group, Inc. International copyrights reserved in all countries. No part of this book may be reproduced in any form without written permission from the publisher. Core Library™ is a trademark and logo of Abdo Publishing.

Printed in the United States of America, North Mankato, Minnesota.
052022
092022

THIS BOOK CONTAINS RECYCLED MATERIALS

Cover Photos: Shutterstock Images, map and icons, fish, duck; Shane Sabin/Shutterstock Images, deer
Interior Photos: Carmen K. Sisson/Cloudybright/Alamy, 4–5; Red Line Editorial, 7 (Mississippi), 7 (USA); Sean Pavone/Shutterstock Images, 9, 45; North Wind Picture Archives/AP Images, 12–13; Michael G. McKinne/Shutterstock Images, 15; Shutterstock Images, 17 (flag), 17 (butterfly), 17 (flower), 17 (alligator); Stubblefield Photography/Shutterstock Images, 17 (bird); Zack Frank/Shutterstock Images, 21, 43; iStockphoto, 24–25; Nina B./Shutterstock Images, 27; Edwin Remsberg/agefotostock/Newscom, 30–31; Michele Crowe/CBS Photo Archive/Getty Images, 36–37

Editor: Angela Lim
Series Designer: Joshua Olson

Library of Congress Control Number: 2021951405

Publisher's Cataloging-in-Publication Data

Names: Hinman, Bonnie, author.
Title: Mississippi / by Bonnie Hinman
Description: Minneapolis, Minnesota : Abdo Publishing, 2023 | Series: Core library of US states | Includes online resources and index.
Identifiers: ISBN 9781532197659 (lib. bdg.) | ISBN 9781098270414 (ebook)
Subjects: LCSH: U.S. states--Juvenile literature. | Southeastern States--Juvenile literature. | Mississippi--History--Juvenile literature. | Physical geography--United States--Juvenile literature.
Classification: DDC 976.2--dc23

Population demographics broken down by race and ethnicity come from the 2019 census estimate. Population totals come from the 2020 census.

CONTENTS

CHAPTER ONE
The Magnolia State................. **4**

CHAPTER TWO
History of Mississippi.............**12**

CHAPTER THREE
Geography and Climate...........**24**

CHAPTER FOUR
Resources and Economy **30**

CHAPTER FIVE
People and Places **36**

Important Dates........................ **42**

Stop and Think......................... **44**

Glossary................................ **46**

Online Resources **47**

Learn More **47**

Index **48**

About the Author....................... **48**

CHAPTER ONE

THE MAGNOLIA STATE

Alligators lurk near the raised walkways at the Gulf Coast Gator Ranch in Moss Point, Mississippi. Visitors follow a trail that lets them walk safely above the alligators. The trail winds through the swamp. Some of the gators glide closer to the walkways. Most rest quietly in the shallow water.

Nearby an airboat buzzes by in the open waters. A family rides on the special boat that moves with a fan. It travels through the reeds

Alligators swim through the swamp at Gulf Coast Gator Ranch in Moss Point, Mississippi.

that stick up above the water. The airboat captain points out gators among the tupelo and cypress trees. The boat captain steers carefully around the big reptiles.

ABOUT MISSISSIPPI

The state of Mississippi is named after the Mississippi River, which forms the western border of the state. Mississippi is nicknamed the Magnolia State. Magnolia trees and their huge, sweetly scented white blossoms are everywhere in Mississippi. In 1900 the Mississippi state government asked schoolchildren to help choose the state flower. The students submitted 23,278 votes. The magnolia was the winner.

Mississippi is located in the southern United States. Tennessee forms the state's northern border, and Alabama lies to the east. Arkansas borders Mississippi to the west. Louisiana makes up part of the western and southern border. The Gulf of Mexico makes up a section of the southern border.

MAP OF MISSISSIPPI

Mississippi has many natural spaces to explore. How does this map help you understand the state's many landscapes?

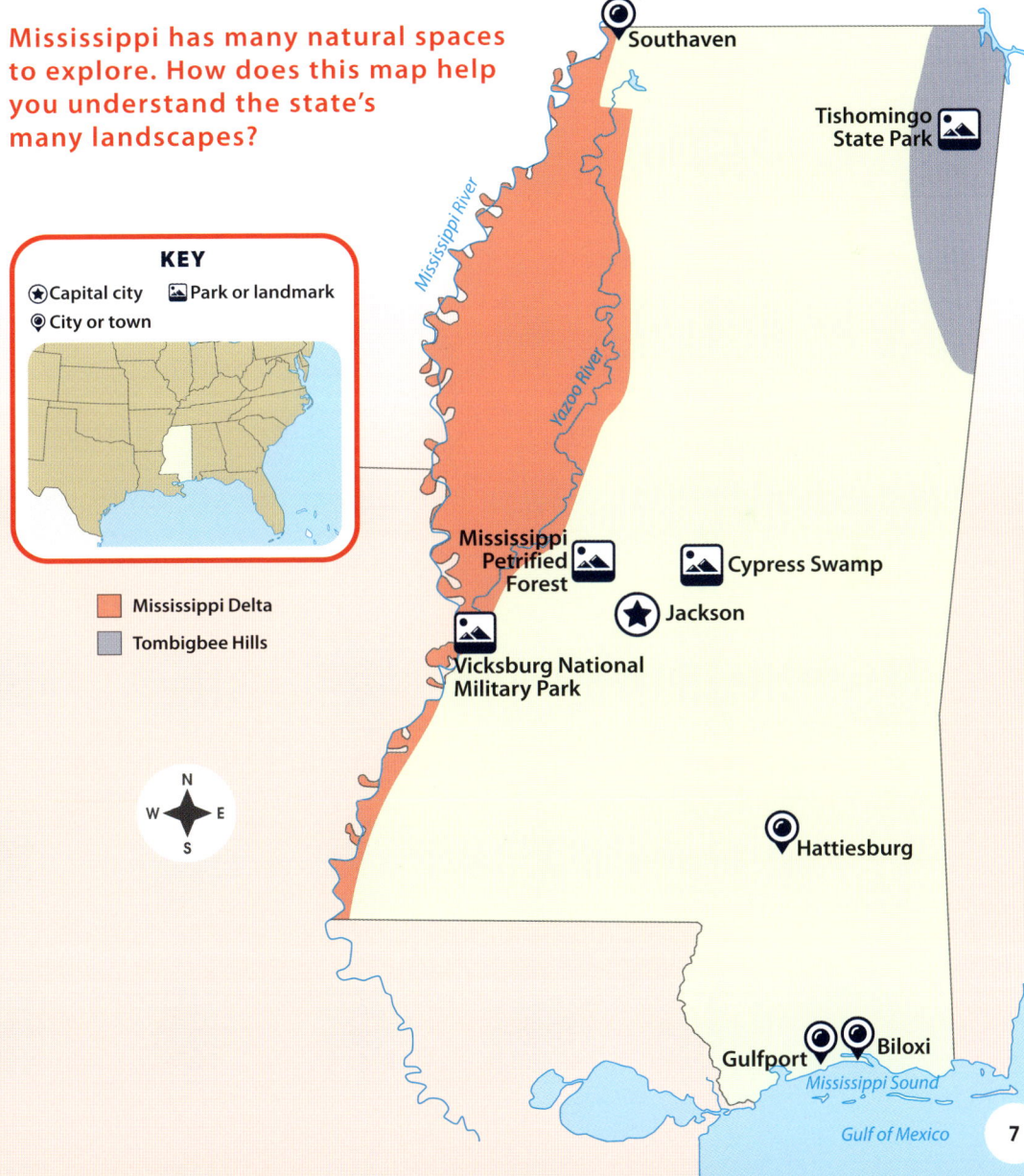

Jackson is the most populated city in Mississippi. It's also the state capital. More than 150,000 people lived in Jackson in 2020. It is an artistic and cultural center with many history museums.

Gulfport is another large city. It is located on the coast of the Mississippi Sound. Biloxi is located nearby. Many of the attractions in this region center on the water. There are miles of beaches to enjoy, and the Institute for Marine Mammal Studies is located there. The institute

PERSPECTIVES

CRUISIN' THE COAST

Cruisin' the Coast began in 1996 as a way to celebrate classic cars. Classic car owners show off their rides as they drive along a 30-mile (48-km) stretch of Highway 90 along the Gulf Coast. They make stops in Mississippi cities such as Gulfport and Ocean Springs. Drivers enjoy food and live music at these locations. Cruisers like Phil Dunaway can't get enough of the event. He said, "The cars, the atmosphere, the eating, we just love the Coast. We love the cars, and we love the people."

The Biloxi Lighthouse is one of the most photographed locations along the Gulf Coast.

cares for sick and injured marine mammals and sea turtles.

Other major cities include Southaven and Hattiesburg. Southaven is located in the northeastern corner of Mississippi. It is a suburb of Memphis, Tennessee. Hattiesburg is often called the Hub City because it is located at the crossroads of six major US highways.

In addition to cities, Mississippi has many kinds of natural beauty that attract tourists. Rivers, streams, and beaches make any kind of water fun possible. Parks and nature preserves teem with birds and other animals. Visitors can stroll through a petrified forest. It features logs that have turned into stone over thousands of years. Many adventures await in Mississippi.

MISSISSIPPI'S PETRIFIED FOREST

The Mississippi Petrified Forest lies just north of Jackson. Millions of years ago, a flood swept down from the northern United States, toppling large trees. These trees washed into a Mississippi ravine, where sand and silt began to cover them. Eventually minerals in the sand and silt caused the trees to turn to stone. Today visitors can walk through the petrified forest and see the ancient remains of trees.

STRAIGHT TO THE
SOURCE

Travel to the Mississippi Gulf Coast is a major part of the state's tourism industry. The COVID-19 pandemic hurt tourism, but the industry began to grow again in 2021 as restrictions eased. Jeffrey Hansell is a restaurant owner in Bay Saint Louis. He spoke of the tourism in the area:

> *I never would have imagined the amount of tourist influx and buzz surrounding our little town. I guess I always took it for granted since I grew up here, but after moving away and coming back, it's obvious what draws them all here. People from all over the Southeast and locals alike seemed to have figured it out because we pack them in every night. And it's not just [Bay Saint Louis], the whole area is seeing [the demand in tourism.]*
>
> Source: Warren Kulo. "Mississippi Coast Enjoying Tourism Boom in Wake of COVID-19 Recovery." *Gulf Live*, 16 July 2021, gulflive.com. Accessed 20 Aug. 2021.

BACK IT UP

The speaker is using evidence to support a point. Write a paragraph describing the point the speaker is making. Then write down two or three pieces of evidence the speaker uses to make the point.

CHAPTER TWO

HISTORY OF MISSISSIPPI

People have lived in the Mississippi region for more than 12,000 years. As the climate in the area warmed, early peoples began building permanent settlements and farming. These lifestyle changes led to the Mississippian period (1000–1550 CE). Peoples of this lifestyle belonged to the Mississippian culture, which first developed in the Mississippi River Valley.

By 1540 many American Indian nations were established in the Mississippi region.

The Natchez confronted the French in order to protect their land.

They included the Choctaw, the Chickasaw, the Natchez, and many others. At this time approximately 200,000 American Indian people lived in present-day Mississippi.

EUROPEANS ARRIVE IN MISSISSIPPI

In 1541 Spanish explorer Hernando de Soto became the first European to enter the Mississippi region. He led an expedition to search for gold and silver. But he did not find any treasures. De Soto and other European explorers introduced diseases that killed many American Indians. In addition they were often violent toward American Indian people.

In 1699 brothers Pierre Le Moyne d'Iberville and Jean-Baptiste Le Moyne, Sieur de Bienville founded Fort Maurepas. It was the first European settlement in Mississippi. Many of the French settlers were fur traders. They traded with American Indian nations such as the Choctaw. Other American Indian nations suffered due to the increasing French presence. For example the

The deep-blue color from indigo is used to dye fabrics.

French attempted to remove the Natchez from the land. This led to the Natchez Massacre (1729–1730). After the massacre, the Natchez no longer existed as a nation. Again, violent conflicts and European diseases killed many American Indians during this period. By 1750 only 16,500 American Indians remained in the Mississippi region.

French settlers also brought some of the first enslaved people to the region. The French forced the enslaved people to grow tobacco and indigo. The region's economy began to rely on labor from enslaved people.

The Mississippi region remained under French control until the end of the French and Indian War (1754–1763). In this war the British fought the French for control of land. The British won and took over most of France's land in North America, including much of present-day Mississippi. Spain maintained control of a small southeastern portion of the Mississippi area.

The British controlled this region for a short time. Then the United States won independence from Great Britain in the Revolutionary War (1775–1783). Mississippi and the surrounding area became part of the new nation. During this time Spanish control in North America weakened. In 1795 the Spanish agreed to give the United States access to the Mississippi River. The river was important for expanding trade. It also encouraged American settlers to move into the region.

The US Congress created the Mississippi Territory in 1798. By 1817 more than 200,000 people lived in the Mississippi Territory. The territory was divided in two.

MISSISSIPPI
QUICK FACTS

Take a closer look at Mississippi's state symbols. How do they help you understand the geography of the state?

Abbreviation: MS
Nickname: The Magnolia State
Motto: *Virtute et armis* (By valor and arms)
Date of statehood: December 10, 1817
Capital: Jackson
Population: 2,961,279
Area: 48,432 square miles (125,438 sq km)

STATE SYMBOLS

State bird
Northern mockingbird

State flower
Magnolia

State butterfly
Spicebush swallowtail

State reptile
American alligator

The western half became the state of Mississippi on December 10, 1817. It was the twentieth US state. An 1819 treaty with Spain gave southeastern Mississippi to the United States.

MISSISSIPPI IN THE 1800s

White settlers continued to move westward. In 1830 the US Congress passed the Indian Removal Act to open more land for American settlers. The act forced many American Indian peoples, including those in Mississippi, from their land. American Indians had to move west of the Mississippi River. The Choctaw were the first Mississippi nation to sign a treaty and move west. Many other nations followed them to what is now Oklahoma. This long journey became known as the Trail of Tears. Thousands of Choctaw people died during the journey. Some Choctaw people remained in Mississippi.

White settlers quickly claimed the lands that had once belonged to American Indian nations. Cotton and other agriculture production increased. Enslaved people labored in cotton fields. Most of them were Black. By the end of the 1830s, approximately 195,000 enslaved people lived in Mississippi.

THE CIVIL WAR

Southern and Northern states were divided on the issue of slavery. The economies of many Southern states, including Mississippi, depended on enslaved people. These states wanted to keep slavery legal. Northern states wanted to abolish the practice.

PERSPECTIVES

PUSHMATAHA

Pushmataha was a Choctaw leader during the 1800s. He sided with the US Army during the War of 1812 (1812–1815). In 1820 the US government created a treaty to force the Choctaw to leave their land. Pushmataha resisted signing the treaty. He traveled with other Choctaw leaders to Washington, DC, to discuss the terms. Pushmataha wanted the US government to provide education for Choctaw youth. He also wanted to make sure that white settlers could not own the new Choctaw land. But Pushmataha became sick and died while in DC. He was buried there with full military honors in the Congressional Cemetery.

President Abraham Lincoln was elected in 1860. He was against slavery. After the election, Southern states seceded from the United States, also called the Union. They formed the Confederacy in part to keep slavery. Mississippi became the second Confederate state on January 9, 1861.

Union and Confederate forces clashed during the American Civil War (1861–1865). Some important battles were fought in Mississippi, such as the Vicksburg Campaign. Vicksburg's location on the Mississippi River made the city an important point to deliver supplies. Both sides fought for control of the city. The Vicksburg Campaign lasted 18 months, ending with a Union victory on July 4, 1863. This cut the Confederacy in half and gave the Union control of the Mississippi River.

The Vicksburg Campaign was a turning point in the Civil War. The Union won the war on April 9, 1865. Formerly enslaved people in the South and throughout the United States were set free. The US government

The Illinois Memorial is one of the most iconic monuments in Vicksburg Military Park. Bronze tablets in the memorial list all the Illinois soldiers who fought in the Vicksburg Campaign.

also passed laws that allowed formerly enslaved people to become citizens and vote.

The US government sent federal troops to southern states, including Mississippi, following the war. This was an attempt to enforce these new laws. Despite these efforts Black people were still not treated equally.

President Rutherford B. Hayes withdrew troops from the South in 1877.

Black Americans faced many forms of discrimination. Mississippi and other southern states required people to pay a tax before they were able to vote. Many Black Americans were unable to pay this fee. Segregation separated Black people and other people of color from white people. Black people had to use separate facilities from white people. Facilities available to Black people were often in worse condition than those available to white people.

CIVIL RIGHTS ERA AND BEYOND

Black people fought for equality. The struggle for civil rights grew in the 1950s and 1960s. In Mississippi, youth led peaceful demonstrations to protest discrimination. Black students and youth groups protested at libraries, parks, and other segregated locations. The efforts of civil rights groups in the South worked. The US government passed a civil rights bill in 1964 that banned discrimination based on race.

Today Mississippi's state government has three branches. The executive branch is the governor and those agencies that work with the governor. The legislative branch writes laws for the state. The judicial branch is the judges and court system. The Mississippi Band of Choctaw Indians is the only federally recognized Indian tribe in Mississippi today.

FREEDOM RIDERS

In 1946 the US Supreme Court ruled that interstate transportation could not be segregated. But this ruling was largely ignored in the South for many years. In 1961 the Congress of Racial Equality sent Black and white Freedom Riders to travel by bus through southern states. Black riders still faced discrimination during interstate transport. The Freedom Riders traveled safely through most states. But they were arrested when they arrived in Jackson. Ultimately the Freedom Ride demonstration paid off. On November 1, 1961, the US government made new policies to end segregation on interstate travel.

CHAPTER THREE

GEOGRAPHY AND CLIMATE

Much of Mississippi consists of flat lowlands. This includes the Gulf Coastal Plain, which covers most of the state. The Gulf Coastal Plain extends throughout the southeastern United States and lies near the Gulf of Mexico. The region has sandy hills, bogs, savannas, and many other landscapes. It is home to many types of animals and plants. Marsh birds such as sandhill cranes live near the coast. Alligators can be found throughout Mississippi but are

Seagrass grows on the white sand beaches at Gulfport.

more common in southern parts of the state. Along the Gulf Coast, shrimp, oysters, and other saltwater species are plentiful.

The Mississippi Delta region in western Mississippi is another lowland area. The Mississippi and Yazoo Rivers in this region carry fertile soil, which makes the area important for agriculture. Catfish, bass, and trout live in the rivers and lakes throughout the state.

Mississippi has few mountains. The Tombigbee Hills are

THE MISSISSIPPI FLYWAY

The Mississippi River is important for many types of birds. It is a habitat for waterbirds such as herons and sandpipers. In addition, nearly 50 percent of North American birds use the Mississippi Flyway to travel. This highway is located in the skies above the Mississippi River. Some birds travel the entire length of the flyway. They fly from northern breeding grounds to the Gulf Coast for the winter. They follow the Mississippi River, where food and shelter are plentiful.

Sandhill cranes are endangered in Mississippi.

at the foothills of the Appalachian Mountains in the northeastern corner of the state. Woodall Mountain lies in these hills. At just 806 feet (246 m) above sea level, it is the highest point in Mississippi. The Tombigbee National Forest is also in this region. It is made mostly of pine trees. More than 62 percent of Mississippi is forested. Many animals live in these woodlands, including black bears and white-tailed deer. Northern mockingbirds and other birds live in the forests. The spicebush swallowtail butterfly is found in wooded swamps.

CLIMATE

Mississippi has long, hot summers that often reach temperatures above 100 degrees Fahrenheit (38°C).

PERSPECTIVES
KUDZU
Kudzu is a climbing vine from Japan. In 1933 the US government decided to plant kudzu to help hold down soil for agriculture. Millions of kudzu seedlings were planted in the southeastern United States, including Mississippi. But the kudzu became invasive. It grows as much as 60 feet (18 m) each year. The vine now covers approximately 500,000 acres (200,000 ha) in Mississippi alone. Andrew Ezell is part of the forestry department at Mississippi State University. "Controlling kudzu is difficult and expensive," he says. Chemicals that kill kudzu can affect soil health and hurt other plants.

Winter temperatures rarely drop below 0 degrees Fahrenheit (−18°C). On average the state receives less than 1 inch (2.5 cm) of snow each year.

Mississippi is one of the wettest US states. Approximately 56 inches (142 cm) of rain falls annually. This warm, wet weather gives Mississippi a growing season of 200 days. In 2011 large amounts of rainfall resulted in massive flooding of the Mississippi River. It was one of the worst recorded floods in US history.

Mississippi agricultural losses totaled $800 million that year.

The state experiences other forms of extreme weather. Thunderstorms are common. Hurricanes can move over the Gulf of Mexico and strike the state. Hurricane Katrina hit the Gulf Coast on August 29, 2005. Mississippi's southern coast was devastated by the storm. Flooding and high winds caused as many as 238 deaths in Mississippi. The storm caused $125 billion in damages in the state.

EXPLORE ONLINE

Chapter Three talks about some of the plants and animals of Mississippi. The article at the website below goes into more detail about this topic. How is the information on the website the same as the information in Chapter Three? What additional information did you learn about Mississippi wildlife?

RIVERS AND STREAMS
abdocorelibrary.com/mississippi

CHAPTER FOUR

RESOURCES AND ECONOMY

Agriculture is the largest industry in Mississippi. The state's farmers take advantage of the fertile soil and the warm and rainy climate. Approximately 29 percent of Mississippi's workforce hold jobs in the agricultural industry. Agriculture brings in $7 billion to the state's economy annually. Soybeans, cotton, and corn are some of Mississippi's top agricultural products. In 2020 the chicken industry brought more than $1 billion to Mississippi. The state ranked fifth

In 1911, young workers who cleaned shrimp for the Biloxi Canning Company posed for a photo. Mississippi aquaculture is still important today.

PERSPECTIVES

IMPROVEMENTS IN CATFISH FARMING

Mississippi raises more catfish than any other state in the country. The flat land and claylike soil in Mississippi are ideal for catfish farms. Several advancements have improved catfish farming. Catfish farmers have bred their catfish to grow more quickly. New medicines protect catfish against diseases. Advanced technology helps maintain oxygen levels in catfish ponds. This helps keep catfish healthy. The new technology is also better for the environment. Will Nobile is a catfish farmer. He said, "I see a real bright future in the catfish business because the younger generation is about healthy, sustainable food."

in chicken and egg production that year.

Aquaculture is another major industry in the state. This includes raising aquatic animals and plants for food. In 2021 Mississippi was the leading state in aquaculture due to its many catfish farms. Other aquaculture products include bass, crawfish, and tilapia.

In addition to agricultural products, Mississippi has natural resources. Vast forests cover the state. As a result, forestry is an important industry in Mississippi. These forests provide wood for construction and furniture. They supply materials for making paper and cardboard. Mississippi also has mines for sand, clay, and gravel throughout the state. These materials are used in construction.

MANUFACTURING AND ENERGY

Manufacturing is a growing industry in Mississippi. Automotive companies such as Nissan and Toyota have manufacturing plants in the state. These companies produce more than 500,000 vehicles each year in Mississippi. Mississippi's low cost of living makes it an attractive location for businesses.

Mississippi is also established in the aerospace industry. The National Aeronautics and Space Administration John C. Stennis Space Center is located in southern Mississippi in Hancock County. It develops and tests rocket engines. Several Mississippi companies make products that are used to make uncrewed aircraft.

> ## PHOBOS
> SpaceX is a space exploration company. Its goal is to create reusable rockets that will allow people to travel to and live on Mars. In 2021 the company moved an offshore oil drilling rig to the coast of Pascagoula, Mississippi, and construction began. SpaceX plans to transform the oil rig into a floating launchpad called Phobos for its spacecraft.

Mississippi also plays an important role in US energy. The state's Chevron plant processes 369,000 barrels of oil every day. In addition the largest single-unit nuclear reactor is in Mississippi.

TOURISM

More than 124,000 people work in Mississippi's tourism industry. Approximately 24.7 million people visited destinations across Mississippi in 2019. Many people visit sites along the Gulf Coast, taking advantage of the region's beaches. But natural beauty can be found throughout the state. Tishomingo State Park is located in northeastern Mississippi. The park boasts scenic views of rolling hills, moss-covered boulders, and fields of wildflowers.

Mississippi cities also attract tourists. Jackson has many historical sites where visitors can learn about civil rights history. The Eudora Welty House in Jackson is a national historic landmark that celebrates the writer. The state also has museums dedicated to music history such as the GRAMMY Museum and the Delta Blues Museum. Mississippi has a growing food scene. Tourists enjoy crawfish boils and other Mississippi foods.

FURTHER EVIDENCE

Chapter Four describes Mississippi agriculture and aquaculture. Why are these industries important? Read the article at the website below. Does the information on the website support facts given about these industries? Does it present new evidence?

MISSISSIPPI RISES TO THE TOP OF US AQUACULTURE

abdocorelibrary.com/mississippi

CHAPTER
FIVE

PEOPLE AND PLACES

Nearly 3 million people lived in Mississippi in 2020. White people who are not Hispanic or Latino make up 60 percent of the population. Approximately 38 percent of Mississippi residents are Black. More than 3 percent of Mississippi residents are Hispanic or Latino. Approximately 1 percent are Asian, and less than 1 percent of the population is American Indian.

Oprah Winfrey, who was born in Mississippi, launched her own television network, the Oprah Winfrey Network, in 2011.

Many famous people were born in Mississippi, including many blues musicians. Big Joe Williams and Bukka White were part of the birth of the blues. Blues music comes from a blend of musical cultures. Some elements originated in Africa and were passed down by enslaved people. Blues music also has influences from white folk music. Mississippi has rich musical traditions. Jackson is nicknamed the City with Soul in part because of its musical history.

Medgar Evers was a famous civil rights activist from Mississippi. He led efforts for Black people

PERSPECTIVES

IDA B. WELLS

Ida B. Wells was born into slavery in Holly Springs, Mississippi, in July 1862. When she was older, Wells became a journalist and activist. She wrote about the violent treatment that many Black Americans faced. Wells called attention to discrimination against Black Americans throughout her life. In addition, Wells was involved in women's rights. She was active in organizations that fought for women's right to vote.

to get the right to vote. He fought against segregation. His wife, Myrlie Evers-Williams, was born in Vicksburg and also fought for civil rights.

Oprah Winfrey was born in rural Mississippi near Kosciusko. She began working in radio and television before hosting her own television show. *The Oprah Winfrey Show* ran for 25 years. Winfrey was the first Black female billionaire in the United States.

PLACES TO VISIT

There are many beautiful places to visit in Mississippi. Visitors can walk along a boardwalk at the Cypress Swamp, known for its bald cypress trees. Water lovers enjoy the longest human-made beach in the United States. The white sand beach runs for 26 miles (42 km) from Biloxi to Henderson Point.

Biloxi is full of history. The Biloxi Lighthouse was completed in 1848. It was famous for having female lighthouse keepers. As visitors climb the 57 steps to the top of the lighthouse, they can see painted waterlines.

EGG BOWL

The Ole Miss Rebels football team plays for the University of Mississippi in Oxford. The Bulldogs represent Mississippi State University in Starkville. Both football teams belong to the Southeastern Conference. They have played a rivalry game against each other since 1944. The game is known as the Egg Bowl. In 2021 it was the tenth-longest uninterrupted series in college football.

These markings show how much water levels rose following major hurricanes from the past 100 years.

History lovers also enjoy the Vicksburg National Military Park. Visitors learn about the Vicksburg Campaign and historic battles of the Civil War. Today the park's more than 1,400 monuments and memorials remember those who fought in the war.

Mississippi is a beautiful state with a long history. Visitors stroll along the Gulf Coast's white sand beaches. They listen to blues music and enjoy eating catfish and seafood. They learn about the nation's history in museums and parks. There is much to see and do while exploring Mississippi.

STRAIGHT TO THE
SOURCE

Tate Taylor is an actor and producer from Jackson. He spoke with the Mississippi Tourism Association about what makes his home state special:

> *We have so many different parts of the state, vastly different both culturally and [geographically] speaking. The Delta is rich with history, great food, [and] big skies. . . . The coast is a seafood [center] and has some beautiful and peaceful spots that feel like they could be anywhere in the world at times. North and east Mississippi are football country, and if you've never been to a college game in Mississippi, you must. The southwest is totally different. Natchez is the oldest city in Mississippi and has influences from Spain, France, and a little bit of New Orleans.*
>
> Source: "Lights! Camera! Mississippi!" *Mississippi Tour Guide*, 2021, mississippitourguide.com. Accessed 3 Sept. 2021.

WHAT'S THE BIG IDEA?
Take a close look at this quote. What does Taylor say about his home state? What does he say about the experiences Mississippi has to offer?

IMPORTANT DATES

More than 12,000 years ago
Early peoples begin living in the Mississippi region.

1541
Hernando de Soto becomes the first European to explore the Mississippi area.

1699
Pierre Le Moyne d'Iberville and Jean-Baptiste Le Moyne, Sieur de Bienville found Fort Maurepas, the first European settlement in present-day Mississippi.

1798
The US Congress creates the Mississippi Territory.

1817
Mississippi becomes the twentieth US state on December 10.

1861
Mississippi becomes the second state to secede from the Union on January 9.

1863
The Union wins the Vicksburg Campaign on July 4.

1865
The American Civil War ends on April 9.

1961
Freedom Riders travel to southern cities, including Jackson, to protest segregation on interstate transportation.

2005
Hurricane Katrina strikes the Gulf Coast, causing as many as 238 deaths in Mississippi.

STOP AND THINK

Dig Deeper

After reading Chapter Two, what questions do you still have about the civil rights movement in Mississippi? With an adult's help, find a few reliable sources that can help you answer your questions. Write a paragraph about what you learned.

Why Do I Care?

Maybe you do not live near the Mississippi River. But that doesn't mean you can't think about why the river is important. How does the river affect Mississippi agriculture and aquaculture? What kinds of animals and plants depend on the river to survive?

You Are There

Chapter Five talks about some of the things to see near Biloxi. Imagine you are visiting the coastal city. Write a letter home telling your friends about your travels. What sites did you visit? What kind of activities did you do? Be sure to add plenty of details to your notes.

Another View

Chapter Three discusses hurricanes and flooding in Mississippi. As you know, every source is different. Ask a librarian or other adult to help you find another source about Mississippi's natural disasters. Write a short essay comparing and contrasting the new source's point of view with that of this book's author. What is the point of view of each author? How are they similar and why? How are they different and why?

GLOSSARY

abolish
to officially end something

activist
a person who takes action to make social or political changes

aerospace
a science related to the sky and outer space

campaign
a series of military battles or attacks

delta
an area of low land formed by a river as it flows into another body of water

discrimination
when people treat others differently based on certain factors such as appearance

fertile
rich in nutrients for growing plants

petrified
turned to stone

secede
to leave a political union

sustainable
able to be used for long periods of time without weakening or running out

ONLINE RESOURCES

To learn more about Mississippi, visit our free resource websites below.

Visit **abdocorelibrary.com** or scan this QR code for free Common Core resources for teachers and students, including vetted activities, multimedia, and booklinks, for deeper subject comprehension.

Visit **abdobooklinks.com** or scan this QR code for free additional online weblinks for further learning. These links are routinely monitored and updated to provide the most current information available.

LEARN MORE

Fabiny, Sarah. *Who Was Ida B. Wells*? Penguin Workshop, 2020.

Rodger, Ellen. *Mississippi River Research Journal*. Crabtree, 2018.

INDEX

aerospace, 33
agriculture, 13, 15, 18–19, 26, 28, 29, 31–32, 35
alligators, 5–6, 17, 25
American Civil War, 20, 40
American Indians, 13–18, 19, 23, 37

beaches, 8, 10, 34, 39–40
Biloxi, 7, 8, 39
blues music, 35, 38, 40

catfish, 26, 32, 40
civil rights, 22–23, 35, 38–39

climate, 13, 27–29, 31
Crusin' the Coast, 8

Evers, Medgar, 38–39

football, 40, 41
forests, 7, 10, 27, 32–33
Fort Maurepas, 14

Gulf of Mexico, 6, 7, 25, 29
Gulfport, 7, 8

Jackson, 7, 8, 10, 17, 23, 35, 38, 41

kudzu, 28

magnolias, 6, 17
manufacturing, 33
Mississippi Sound, 7, 8

Natchez Massacre, 15

Pushmataha, 19

slavery, 15, 18–21, 38

tourism, 10, 11, 34–35, 41
Trail of Tears, 18

Wells, Ida B., 38
Winfrey, Oprah, 39

About the Author

Bonnie Hinman lives in southwestern Missouri with her husband, Bill, and near her children and grandchildren. Hinman has written more than 65 books for kids.